STUDY GI

SET YOUR KIDS UP FOR FUTURE SUCCESS

RAISING PARENTS

For foreign and subsidiary rights, contact the author.

Cover design: Sara Young
Cover photo: Andrew van Tilborgh

ISBN: 978-1-957369-98-3   1 2 3 4 5 6 7 8 9 10

Printed in the United States of America

STUDY GUIDE

SET YOUR KIDS UP FOR FUTURE SUCCESS

RAISING PARENTS

JONATHAN BROZOZOG

WITH JOANNE BROZOZOG

ARROWS & STONES

CONTENTS

SET YOUR KIDS UP FOR FUTURE SUCCESS

RAISING PARENTS

JONATHAN BROZOZOG

WITH JOANNE BROZOZOG

WISDOM AND UNDERSTANDING

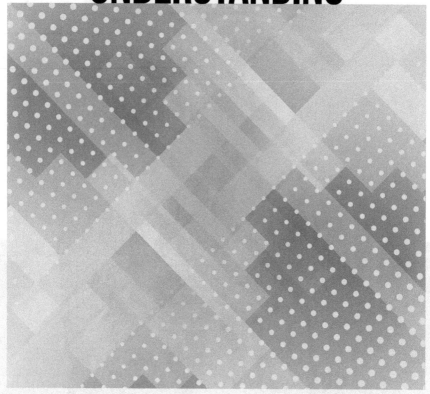

"Sometimes, people just have to get knowledge and wisdom through the painful and slow process of experience."

REVIEW, REFLECT, AND RESPOND:

As you read
Chapter 1:
"Wisdom and
Understanding"
in *Raising
Parents*, review,
reflect on,
and respond
to the text by
answering
the following
questions.

In your own words, what is wisdom? Where
do you go for wisdom?

_____

_____

_____

_____

_____

_____

_____

_____

_____

_____

Where else can you go for wisdom? Is there
a shortcut for obtaining more?

_____

_____

_____

_____

_____

_____

_____

_____

_____

_____

_____

_____

Consider the scripture above and answer the following questions:

What stands out to you from this verse? What does it look like to manage one's family well?

_____

_____

_____

_____

_____

_____

_____

How do you manage your family well and get your children to obey you "in a manner worthy of full respect"? What do you think this means?

_____

_____

_____

_____

_____

_____

_____

_____

_____

_____

In your own words, why is parenting so important?

_____

_____

_____

_____

_____

_____

_____

_____

Where do you go to get insight on how to parent effectively? What other resources are available to you?

_____

_____

_____

_____

_____

_____

_____

_____

What's the difference between being qualified to parent and being called to parent? Which are you? What does this imply?

_____

_____

_____

_____

_____

_____

_____

_____

_____

_____

Do you have godly counsel in your life that can assist you when you don't know how to handle a particular situation? Who is part of this counsel?

_____

_____

_____

_____

_____

_____

_____

_____

What makes a perfect parent? Is this achievable? Why or why not?

_____

_____

_____

_____

_____

_____

_____

_____

_____

A HEALTHY HOME

"Seeds just do better if they have the right kind of soil, climate, and attention from a caring cultivator . . . and so do children. Environment matters!"

READING
TIME

As you read
Chapter 2: "A
Healthy Home"
in *Raising
Parents*, review,
reflect on,
and respond
to the text by
answering
the following
questions.

REVIEW, REFLECT, AND RESPOND:

What does a healthy home look like? List
the key elements and cornerstones of a
healthy home.

_____

_____

_____

_____

_____

_____

Taking the elements you listed above into
consideration, do you have a healthy home?
What's missing?

_____

_____

_____

_____

_____

What do you think the advantages are of
having a healthy home? Who benefits?

_____

_____

_____

_____

_____

That is why a man leaves his father and mother and is united to his wife, and they become one flesh.

Genesis 2:24 (NIV)

Consider the scripture above and answer the following questions:

What do you think happens if a man goes against this verse and leaves his father and mother prematurely for someone to whom they are not yet married?

_____

_____

_____

_____

_____

_____

_____

_____

What does this verse mean when it says, "they become one flesh"? What does "one flesh" really signify?

_____

_____

_____

_____

_____

_____

_____

_____

What seeds are you currently sowing into your children's lives? Are any of these seeds negative? What positive seeds would you like to sow?

_____

_____

_____

_____

_____

_____

How can you ensure your home environment will make a child's heart (the soil) accept and grow the seeds you sow?

_____

_____

_____

_____

_____

_____

What is the cornerstone of your household? Is it Jesus, or something else? Do you believe this is evident in how you live, act, communicate and parent?

_____

_____

_____

_____

_____

_____

Why do you think the statement, "children are the by-products of marriage, not a replacement for it, or the completion of it," is so important to believe? Have you ever fallen into thinking that children *are* a replacement for or a completion of marriage?

_____

_____

_____

_____

_____

_____

_____

_____

_____

_____

Describe what being "one flesh" means in your own words.

_____

_____

_____

_____

_____

_____

_____

_____

_____

_____

_____

_____

EFFECTIVE PARENTING

"If you expose your kids to all sorts of enriching experiences yet fail to teach them the greater value of family relationships, you could be unintentionally setting them up for sorrow and failure in the things that matter most."

READING TIME

As you read Chapter 3: "Effective Parenting" in *Raising Parents*, review, reflect on, and respond to the text by answering the following questions.

REVIEW, REFLECT, AND RESPOND:

What makes an effective parent in your book? What are the key traits all effective parents possess?

_____

_____

_____

_____

_____

_____

What valuable parenting lessons have you learned recently that have helped you become a more effective parent?

_____

_____

_____

_____

_____

What do you think is the biggest limitation holding parents back from being effective?

_____

_____

_____

_____

_____

Consider the scripture above and answer the following questions:

What stands out to you from this verse in Hebrews? Is any of this applicable to your family life?

_____

_____

_____

_____

_____

_____

_____

_____

Why do you think Paul mentions meeting together in his letter to the Hebrews? What are the advantages of meeting together?

_____

_____

_____

_____

_____

_____

_____

What is the "biggest problem" with both parents and children discussed in this chapter? Do you fall victim to this problem at all? How so?

_____

_____

_____

_____

_____

_____

_____

_____

_____

_____

Have you found yourself—or a family member—putting activities above relationships in your life? Describe the situation. How did this make other family members feel?

_____

_____

_____

_____

_____

_____

_____

_____

_____

_____

_____

_____

In your household, do you think relationships or activities hold a higher value in your children's lives?

_____

_____

_____

_____

_____

_____

How often do you and your entire family sit down together for a meal? Do you want this to be more frequently than it is now?

_____

_____

_____

_____

_____

_____

Do you feel grandparents are essential in the lives of children? How often do your children get to see their grandparents?

_____

_____

_____

_____

_____

_____

_____

THINGS THAT DIVIDE

"Families have issues because the individuals within these families have them."

READING TIME

As you read
Chapter 4:
"Things That
Divide" in
Raising Parents,
review, reflect
on, and respond
to the text by
answering
the following
questions.

REVIEW, REFLECT, AND RESPOND:

What do you think are common factors that divide and separate families?

_____

_____

_____

_____

_____

_____

What has divided your family in the past? Is it still divided over anything?

_____

_____

_____

_____

_____

_____

Once a family is divided, how can one bridge the division?

_____

_____

_____

_____

_____

_____

> *"You have heard that is was said to the people long ago, 'You shall not murder, and anyone who murders will be subject to judgment.' But I tell you that anyone who is angry with a brother or sister will be subject to judgment. Again, anyone who says to a brother or sister, 'Raca,' is answerable to the court. And anyone who says, 'You fool!' will be in the danger of the fire of hell."*
>
> *Matthew 5:21-22 (NIV)*

Consider the scripture above and answer the following questions:

What stands out from this verse to you, and why?

_____

_____

_____

_____

_____

When was the last time you were angry with a brother or sister? Why were you angry?

_____

_____

_____

_____

_____

_____

Do you think it is fair to receive judgment for the anger you listed above? Why or why not?

_____

_____

_____

_____

_____

_____

_____

_____

What has divided your family in the past, and how did you over-
come the issue? Did you learn anything from this experience?

_____

_____

_____

_____

_____

Why can offenses be so dangerous in family life? What happens if
they go unaddressed?

_____

_____

_____

_____

_____

Consider the different types of walls discussed (offense, fear, mis-
trust, and bitterness). Which do you feel your family struggles with
the most?

_____

_____

_____

_____

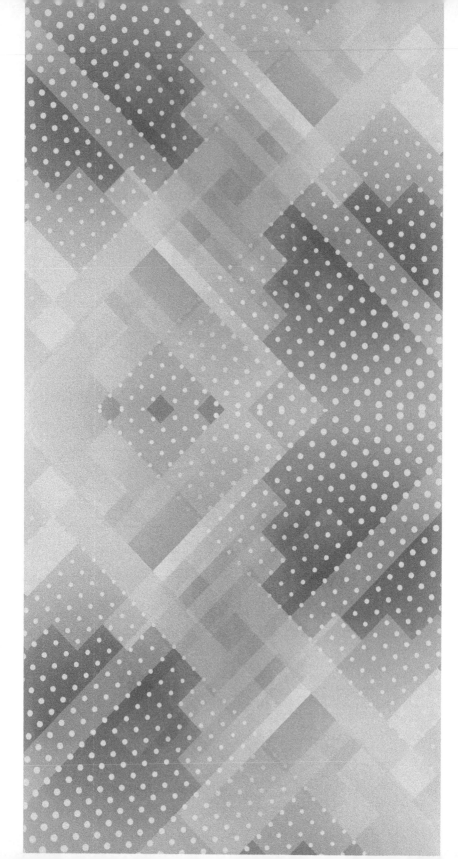

_____

_____

_____

_____

Do you exhibit both of the non-negotiables discussed in this
chapter (honesty and be graciousness)? How do you know?

_____

_____

_____

_____

_____

_____

_____

How do you manage conflict in the home? Do you find this to
be effective? How can you improve and handle disagreements
more effectively?

_____

_____

_____

_____

_____

_____

_____

AN ATMOSPHERE OF PEACE

"Without peace, there can be no realistic hope of maintaining the type of environment for children (or adults) that is conducive to healthy growth in faith and in interpersonal relationships."

READING TIME

As you read Chapter 5: "An Atmosphere of Peace" in *Raising Parents*, review, reflect on, and respond to the text by answering the following questions.

REVIEW, REFLECT, AND RESPOND:

How would you describe an atmosphere of peace? What would this look like in the home?

_____

_____

_____

_____

_____

_____

_____

Do you consider your household to have an atmosphere of peace? Was it always like this?

_____

_____

_____

_____

_____

Do you think peace is a result of being intentional, or does it come about by chance? Explain your answer.

_____

_____

_____

_____

_____

_____

> *But the fruit of the Spirit is love, joy, peace, forbearance, kindness, goodness, faithfulness, gentleness and self-control. Against such things there is no law.*
>
> *Galatians 5:22 (NIV)*

Consider the scripture above and answer the following questions:

Which of the fruits of the Spirit is present and tangible in your home? Which do you most need to work on?

_____

_____

_____

_____

_____

_____

_____

_____

Do you think all the fruits of the Spirit are necessary for an atmosphere of peace?

_____

_____

_____

_____

_____

_____

_____

_____

_____

Why do you feel it is important to recognize God is a God of peace and order? Do you think this will help you establish peace in your home?

_____

_____

_____

_____

_____

_____

_____

_____

What does genuine peace look like in the home? Does it mean quietness, no activity, and no commotion? Explain your answer.

_____

_____

_____

_____

_____

_____

_____

_____

Do you think disagreement is inherently negative? Why or why not?

_____

_____

_____

_____

_____

_____

_____

_____

_____

_____

_____

_____

_____

What's the difference between being a peacekeeper and a peace-maker? How does one make peace?

_____

_____

_____

_____

_____

_____

_____

_____

_____

_____

_____

_____

_____

HONOR AND GRACE

"Our children will need to learn how to live in ways that are contrary to the rebellious culture that surrounds them and contrary to their own sinful inclinations. Grace and discipline will be needed along the way."

As you read
Chapter 6:
"Honor and
Grace" in
Raising Parents,
review, reflect
on, and respond
to the text by
answering
the following
questions.

REVIEW, REFLECT, AND RESPOND:

What are the guiding principles of your household?

_____

_____

_____

_____

_____

_____

What made you choose these principles?

_____

_____

_____

_____

_____

How do you raise your children with honor and grace? What happens if these two elements are not in the home?

_____

_____

_____

_____

_____

_____

_____

> *"Honor your father and your mother, so that you may live
> long in the land the LORD your God has given you."*
>
> *Exodus 20:12 (NIV)*

Consider the scripture above and answer the following questions:

How can children honor their father and mother?

_____

_____

_____

_____

_____

What would dishonoring one's father and mother look like? What
do you think would cause this?

_____

_____

_____

_____

_____

According to this verse—which was stated to the Israelites—why
should children honor their father and mother?

_____

_____

_____

_____

_____

_____

_____

_____

What are the most important "commandments" of your family's household? Why did you choose these?

_____

_____

_____

_____

_____

_____

_____

Which do you feel is more important: respect or obedience? Explain your answer.

_____

_____

_____

_____

_____

_____

What can we learn from Jesus Christ's life in this area?

_____

_____

_____

_____

_____

How would you describe the culture of your home? Be specific.

_____

_____

_____

_____

_____

_____

_____

_____

_____

How many of the seven signs of a healthy home listed towards the end of the chapter does your household display? Which do you need to work on?

_____

_____

_____

_____

_____

_____

_____

_____

_____

WHY GODLY DISCIPLINE?

"When God disciplines His children, He does so with a redemptive purpose in mind."

READING
TIME

As you read
Chapter 7:
"Why Godly
Discipline?" in
Raising Parents,
review, reflect
on, and respond
to the text by
answering
the following
questions.

REVIEW, REFLECT, AND RESPOND:

How do you discipline in your household?
Was this the same type of discipline you
were raised with as a child?

_____

_____

_____

_____

_____

_____

What do you think is the difference between
discipline and godly discipline?

_____

_____

_____

_____

_____

Do you think disciplining can have an adverse
effect on children when done incorrectly? Can
you give an example of this occurring?

_____

_____

_____

_____

_____

_____

> *In your struggle against sin, you have not yet resisted to the point of shedding your blood. And have you completely forgotten this word of encouragement that addresses you as a father addresses his son? It says, "My son, do not make light of the Lord's discipline, and do not lose heart when he rebukes you, because the Lord disciplines the one he loves, and he chastens everyone he accepts as his son."*
>
> *Hebrews 12:4-6 (NIV)*

Consider the scripture above and answer the following questions:

What does this verse reveal to you about the Lord's discipline?

_____

_____

_____

_____

_____

Why is the fact that "the Lord disciplines the one he loves" so important to recognize?

_____

_____

_____

_____

Do you feel your discipline as a parent should replicate God's discipline of His children? Why or why not?

_____

_____

_____

_____

_____

_____

_____

In your own words, define disobedience, dishonor, and disrespect.

_____

_____

_____

_____

_____

_____

_____

If the above behaviors are displayed in your household by your children, do you discipline them? How?

_____

_____

_____

_____

How can you exhibit both justice and mercy to your children? How do you personally balance the two?

_____

_____

_____

_____

_____

Do you think discipline is one-size-fits-all, or does each child need to be disciplined differently?

_____

_____

_____

_____

_____

_____

What does transitional parenting mean? How have you transitioned as a parent as your child grows older and changes?

_____

_____

_____

_____

_____

_____

Is your parenting guided by the two immutable principles given at the end of this chapter? What do you think occurs when parents do not follow these guidelines?

_____

_____

_____

_____

_____

_____

_____

CORRECTING OUR KIDS

"Effective discipline includes the pursuit of techniques that work as well as the avoidance of techniques that don't work."

REVIEW, REFLECT, AND RESPOND:

READING TIME

As you read Chapter 8: "Correcting Our Kids" in *Raising Parents*, review, reflect on, and respond to the text by answering the following questions.

What does "age-appropriate discipline" mean? How do you think discipline should evolve as a child grows into adulthood?

_____

_____

_____

_____

_____

_____

What are some disciplinary techniques you've stopped using due to lack of effectiveness?

_____

_____

_____

_____

_____

Are there any new disciplinary techniques you practice now that you didn't when your children were younger?

_____

_____

_____

_____

_____

_____

> *Fathers, do not exasperate your children; instead, bring*
> *them up in the training and instruction of the Lord.*
>
> *Exodus 6:4 (NIV)*

Consider the scripture above and answer the following questions:

What do you think this verse means when it tells fathers not to "exasperate" their offspring?

_____

_____

_____

_____

_____

Do you feel you and your partner are bringing up your children in the training and instruction of the Lord, as this verse commands?

_____

_____

_____

_____

_____

What do you think is more important: how discipline is administered (the form it takes), or the motivation behind it? Explain your answer.

_____

_____

_____

_____

_____

What is the difference between positive and negative reinforcement? Which do you think is more effective?

_____

_____

_____

_____

_____

_____

Do you use both these forms of discipline? Which do you use more commonly? What situation(s) brings you to utilize the form you use less frequently?

_____

_____

_____

_____

_____

_____

Do you ever threaten discipline and then not follow through? Do you think this may cause trust-related issues?

_____

_____

_____

_____

_____

_____

CHAPTER 9

THE SPOKEN WORD

"Words can be just as destructive as they are inspiring. . . . just as deadly as they are life-giving."

Recall a time when the words someone said to you inspired, motivated, or positively influenced you. What did they say, and what was the result?

_____

_____

_____

_____

_____

_____

Think of another time when the words someone said were destructive and hurt you. What did they say, and why did it hurt?

_____

_____

_____

_____

_____

_____

Do you watch the type of words you say around your children? Why?

_____

_____

_____

_____

_____

_____

> *But I tell you that everyone will have to give account on the day of judgment for every empty word they have spoken.*
>
> *Matthew 12:36*

Consider the scripture above and answer the following questions:

What do you draw from this verse? Does it change the way you think and speak?

_____

_____

_____

_____

_____

What is an "empty word"? Are these common for us today?

_____

_____

_____

_____

If you were told every word you or your family spoke would end up online the next day, would you be more careful about what you say? What would you change or warn your family not to ever say?

_____

_____

_____

_____

How can you fill the role of both priest and prophet in the lives of your children? What does this mean practically?

_____

_____

_____

_____

_____

How does letting our children fail actually help them succeed? Do you let your children fail? How so?

_____

_____

_____

_____

How often do you verbally reward your children when they do something right?

_____

_____

_____

_____

Do you reward them as often as you discipline them? Why or why not?

_____

_____

_____

_____

THOSE DEFIANT YEARS

"Once a child reaches puberty, he or she will begin to subconsciously decide what parts of the parent's teaching to keep and what parts to abandon."

READING TIME

As you read Chapter 10: "Those Defiant Years" in *Raising Parents*, review, reflect on, and respond to the text by answering the following questions.

Have your children reached their "defiant years"? If yes, what is this like for them and for you?

_____

_____

_____

_____

_____

_____

Do you remember your defiant years as a child? Do you see glimpses of your defiant younger self in your children? How so?

_____

_____

_____

_____

_____

_____

_____

At what point does defiance go too far? How do you respond when this occurs?

_____

_____

_____

_____

_____

_____

> *Above all else, guard your heart, for*
> *everything you do flows from it.*
>
> *Proverbs 4:23*

Consider the scripture above and answer the following questions:

Of all verses, why do you think this is such an important one to teach your children?

_____

_____

_____

_____

_____

How does one guard their heart? What does this look like in action?

_____

_____

_____

_____

_____

When this verse states "everything you do flows from it," does it really mean EVERYTHING?

_____

_____

_____

_____

_____

How do you feel technology and the internet contribute to a child's defiance? What can you do to limit this external influence without completely isolating your child?

_____

_____

_____

_____

_____

_____

What is your stance on your children dating? Why do you believe this is the best stance to take?

_____

_____

_____

_____

_____

_____

Do you voice the value of vision to your children? Why is this important?

_____

_____

_____

_____

_____

_____

Do you find sexual orientation to be a difficult area of parenting to explain and navigate? If so, why? If not, what helps you navigate this area?

_____

_____

_____

_____

_____

_____

_____

_____

_____

What is the church's role in parenting? Do you let the church fulfill this role with your children? How so?

_____

_____

_____

_____

_____

_____

_____

_____

_____

Lightning Source UK Ltd.
Milton Keynes UK
UKHW050915240123
415815UK00022B/600